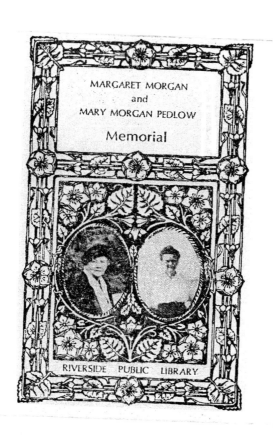

MARGARET MORGAN
and
MARY MORGAN PEDLOW

Memorial

RIVERSIDE PUBLIC LIBRARY

Mapping the World

Mapping the World

Walter Oleksy

Franklin Watts
A Division of Scholastic Inc.
New York • Toronto • London • Auckland • Sydney
Mexico City • New Delhi • Hong Kong
Danbury, Connecticut

Note to readers: Definitions for words in **bold** can be found in the Glossary at the back of this book.

Photographs © 2002: AKG London: 2, 17; AP/Wide World Photos/Jim McKnight: cover; Art Resource, NY: 16 (Scala/Biblioteca Nazionale, Florence, Italy), 28; Bridgeman Art Library International Ltd., London/New York: 37 (British Library, London), 12 (Giraudon/Louvre, Paris, France), 30 (Harriet Wynter Antiques, London), 14 (Index/Bibliotheque Nationale, Paris, France), 25 (The Royal Institution, London, UK); Corbis Images: 5 left, 21, 29 (Archivo Iconografico, S.A.), 15, 41 (Bettman), 38 (Hulton-Deutsch Collection), 48 (Roger Ressmeyer), 40 (Galen Rowell), 6 (Julia Waterlow; Eye Ubiquitous), 20, 26; Culver Pictures: 10, 32; Mary Evans Picture Library: 19; North Wind Picture Archives: 9, 22, 34; PhotoEdit: 46 (Mark Richards), 5 right, 44; Photri Inc.: 42; Superstock, Inc./A.K.G. Berlin: 11; Visuals Unlimited/Mark Gibson: 47.

The illustration on the cover shows a mapmaker at work. The photograph opposite the title page shows a painting by Vermeer entitled *The Geographer*.

Library of Congress Cataloging-in-Publication Data

Oleksy, Walter G., 1930–
    Mapping the world / by Walter Oleksy.
        p. cm. — (Watts library)
    Includes bibliographical references and index.
    ISBN 0-531-12029-5 (lib. bdg.)   0-531-16636-8 (pbk.)
    1. Cartography—History—Juvenile literature. [1. Cartography—History. 2. Maps.] I. Title. II. Series.
GA105.6 .O377 2001
912—dc21   2001017562

Contents

Many historians believe that Chinese civilization began along the banks of the Yellow River.

Chapter One

Mapping in Ancient Times

Maps made exploration of regions, then continents, and finally the whole world possible. In ancient China, civilization began on the shores of the Yellow River in about 1600 B.C. As this civilization grew and evolved, there was an increased need to explore and learn more about the geography of this vast country. Three main factors—war between rival states and with invaders, the search for wisdom inside and outside its borders, and trade —drove interest in creating maps.

First Printed Map

The first known printed map was made in China in about A.D. 1155. This was more than three hundred years before printed maps appeared in Europe.

The first Chinese explorer was Zhang Qian. In 115 B.C., Han emperor Wu Di sent him to the Wu-Sun people in central Asia, to forge a military alliance against their common enemy, the Huns. The route that Zhang Qian took on his travels became known as the Silk Road, a roughly charted but major trade route from Asia to Europe.

Along with exploration, religion played an important role in mapping routes for the ancient Chinese. **Buddhism**, which originated in India during the 500s B.C., spread to China in about the 200s B.C. Chinese members of this religion would journey to India to visit Buddhist shrines. In the course of making their pilgrimages, the ancient Chinese created routes between China and India.

Mapping the Ancient World

Exploration came naturally to the ancient Greeks, since their nation was located between Europe and Asia, bounded by the waters of the Aegean and Mediterranean Seas. Coastal trade by sea among Greek city-states flourished for many years. During the 700s B.C., pilgrims were sent by ship to establish new colonies along the Mediterranean and Black Seas. They also journeyed to present-day Italy and France. This sea commerce and colonization led to the gathering of geographic information later used in charts of Mediterranean coastlines and then in more detailed maps.

Hecataeus of Miletus, who lived around the time of 500 B.C., wrote a book about the geography and customs of the

First Greek Map of the World

The first Greek map of the world was compiled by the philosopher Anaximander. He also wrote a history of the universe. Historians believe that he lived from approximately 610 to 545 B.C.

world known to the ancient Greeks. He divided the world into two parts—Europe and Asia. Another early Greek writer, Herodotus, traveled widely in the Middle East and into Egypt. In 444 B.C. he wrote about his travels in a book called *The Histories*. It included reports of land and sea expeditions he got from sailors and traders, which became of great value to future mapmakers and globe makers. Herodotus would become known as the father of history.

Alexander the Great, king of Macedonia, led his armies as far as Egypt. During his conquest of the Persian Empire he explored much of Asia. He took with him scholars and geographers to study and map the regions he conquered.

This map shows the geography of the world according to Herodotus.

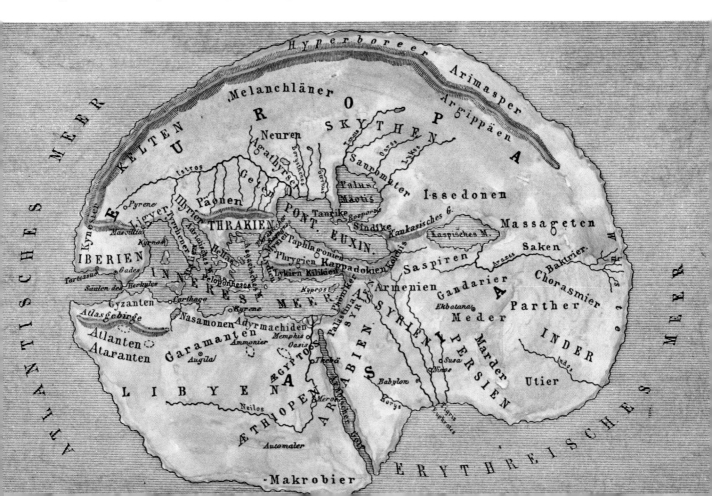

In 300 B.C., another Greek adventurer, Pytheas, sailed from present-day Marseilles in France to the unknown north country. He is believed to have **circumnavigated** the British Isles, crossed the North Sea, and reached Norway and Iceland, which he considered to be the northern limit of the world. The Pythean voyages began to convince geographers that the world was much larger than was originally thought.

Rough maps were made of these wanderings to distant lands, but they were inaccurate because of a lack of both detail and scientific knowledge of mapmaking. **Globes** also were made by Greek philosophers in the fifth and fourth centuries B.C., based on the theory that the Earth was a sphere. Amazingly, Eratosthenes of Cyrene's third century B.C. globe of the world was accurate to within 5 percent of its true size.

Roman Geographers

By the second century A.D., the Roman Empire extended from northern Britain southeast through Europe to the Persian Gulf and Egypt and along the north coast of Africa. Romans explored of much of Europe, from Spain to Britain. They surveyed and created land routes over the Alps to connect their conquered lands with Rome.

Several Roman expeditions seeking geographic knowledge extended from the north coast of Africa into the unexplored interior. By A.D. 97, Chinese merchants brought their silks to the Roman city of Antioch. Romans then followed the silk trade routes to journey into central Asia.

Roman exploration was driven by their desire for treasure, conquest, and geographic knowledge. Julius Caesar wanted both to enlarge the Roman Empire and to have the lands therein explored. Emperor Nero sent explorers to learn the source of the Nile River in Africa.

This map shows the territories of the Roman Empire.

Ptolemy's **Geography** *influenced maps and mapmakers for centuries.*

Chapter Two

World Maps Evolve

In the second century A.D., Ptolemy, a Greek astronomer and mathematician, compiled in his *Geography* all the then-known writings of world exploration. His publication was called a **gazetteer**, which is a geographical dictionary. It contained maps and more than eight thousand place names from Scotland to Malaya.

The gazetteer also showed geographical features such as lakes, rivers, mountains, and deserts. Ptolemy estimated the

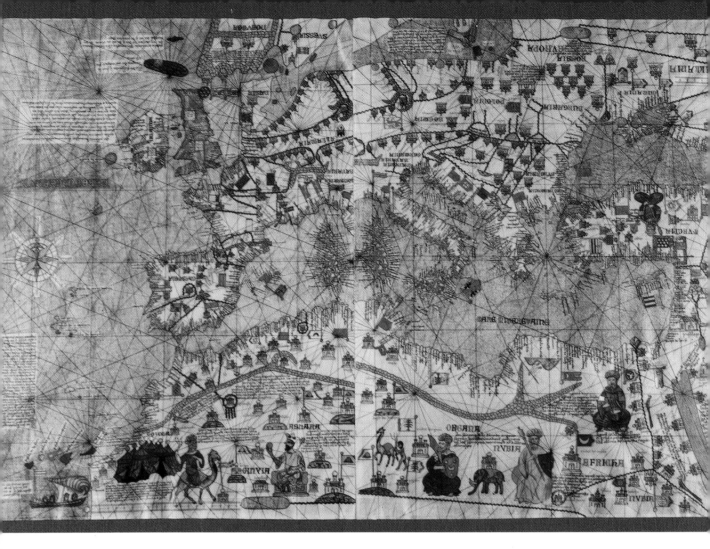

This portolan chart shows North Africa and Europe. It was part of an atlas published in 1375.

geographical coordinates of these features, measuring **longitude** eastward from the Fortunate Islands, the farthest westward place in the then-known world. Some of the information in Ptolemy's gazetteer was of questionable accuracy, obtained from traders, sailors, and adventurers unskilled in mapping.

Another next step forward in mapmaking occurred in the 1200s in Italy and Spain when the first **portolan charts** were made. *Portolan* means "written sailing directions" in Italian. The sea charts were probably first made by sailors to navigate

14

along the Mediterranean coast. They drew a mesh of crisscrossed lines on sheepskins to find their way from harbor to harbor.

Ptolemy's world map, all but forgotten over the years by the West, was known in Byzantium. The West rediscovered Ptolemy's work in the 1300s when Turkey invaded Byzantium, the eastern part of the Roman Empire. The Greek writings of Ptolemy were among the treasures refugees took with them when they fled for safety. After being smuggled to Florence, Italy, they were translated into Latin in about 1410. European geographers and other scholars were amazed at the knowledge in Ptolemy's world maps.

The Age of Exploration

Soon after the invention of the printing press, demand for printed maps developed. One of the first European printed maps was St. Isidore's T-O map, a type of circular map, printed in Augsburg, Germany, in 1472. This map showed Africa to be larger than all the other land

Dog-Headed Cannibals

The Venetian merchant-adventurer, Marco Polo, was one of the most well-traveled men in history because of his journeys to China and India between 1271 and 1296. He later wrote about his travels, sharing his vast knowledge of Eastern and Asian geography with future mapmakers. But some doubted his accuracy because he also wrote about seeing creatures such as dog-headed cannibals on the Andaman Islands in the seas south of India and west of Burma. A scene from Polo's account of the canine cannibals appears in a painting on Pierre Desceliers's World Map of 1550.

areas of the known world combined. However, that map was soon forgotten when multiple copies of Ptolemy's map were printed and found their way to sea captains and explorers.

One of these was a Florentine astronomer-mathematician, Paolo dal Pozzo Toscanelli. He saw the map's potential for increasing world geographic knowledge if sea captains used the map to sail to distant and unexplored lands. Toscanelli drew upon Ptolemy's map to create one of his own in 1474. He sent a copy to a young adventurer named Christopher Columbus, encouraging him to sail beyond the western end of

Based on the work of Ptolemy, Toscanelli created his own map of the world.

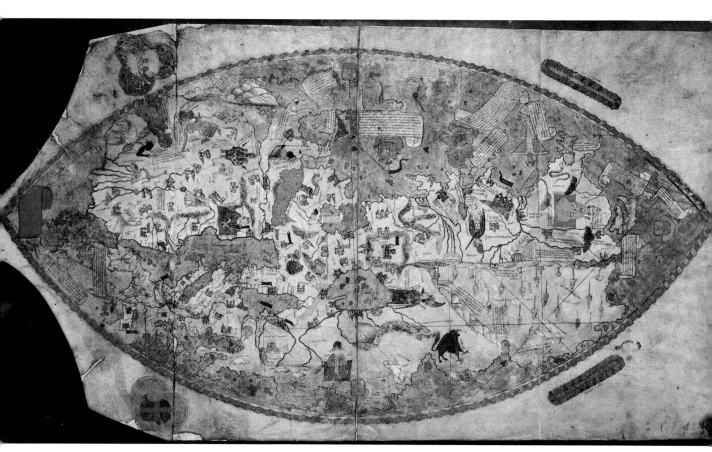

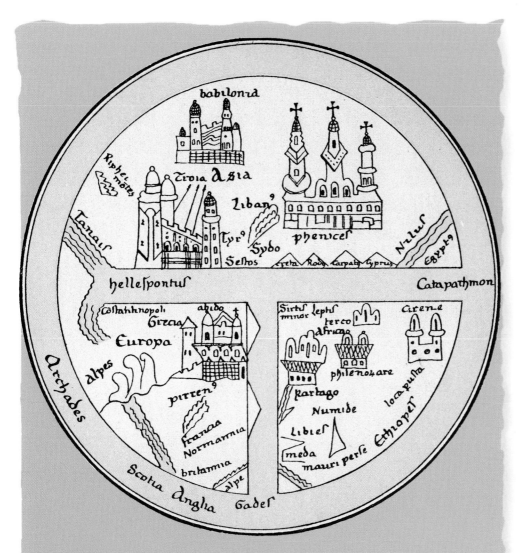

T-O Maps

So-called T-O maps of the world were popular in the Middle Ages. These maps reflected Christian belief at the time that Jerusalem was at the center of the world. East was at the top, surrounded by a circular ocean (the O). The continents of Europe, Asia, and Africa were separated by the arms of the T representing the Mediterranean to east and west, the Nile River to the south, and the River Don flowing into the Black Sea to the north.

the Mediterranean Sea where he would find a western sea route to the East.

Columbus used the Toscanelli map on his voyage of discovery of the Americas. He reached San Salvador in the Bahamas on October 12, 1492, thinking he had landed in China. The reason for the error in belief was that Toscanelli's map repeated Ptolemy's inaccurate estimate of the size of the world.

Three sketch maps of the *Mondo Novo*—which means "New World"—believed to have been made by Columbus and another Portuguese navigator of his time, Bartholomeu Dias, are now in the Biblioteca Nazionale in Florence, Italy. Also, a map showing the Americas drawn by Giovanni Contarini in 1506 still exists.

In 1507, Martin Waldseemüller created a very important world map that included the Americas. He labeled some of the new lands discovered across the Atlantic Ocean as America on his map. This is considered the first recorded use of the name on a map. He picked the name to honor Amerigo Vespucci, the Italian navigator. Waldseemüller's America was only the South American continent, not the entire Americas.

The Age of Exploration moved ahead rapidly after Columbus's voyages, as new knowledge of the geography of the lands to the west of Europe led to creation of new and more accurate maps. Another important contribution to the knowledge of world geography was the voyage begun by Portuguese navigator Ferdinand Magellan that resulted in the first

Globe of the Modern World

A German navigator, Martin Behaim, created the first globe in the modern Western world in 1492. Since it was made before Columbus's famous expedition, there is no mention of the Americas on the globe.

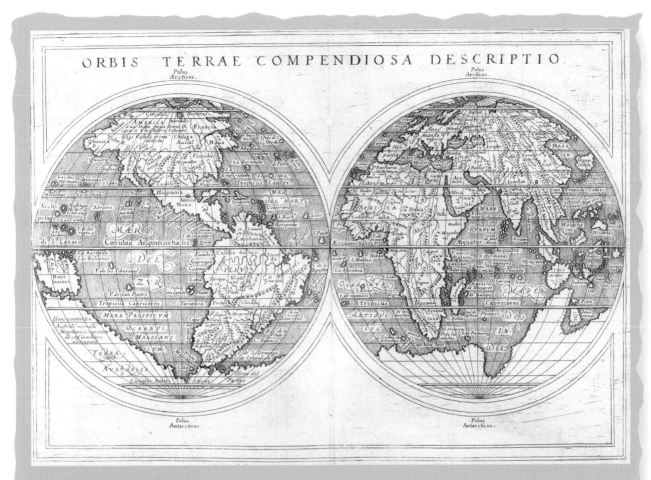

Gerardus Mercator

A Flemish **cartographer**, Gerardus Mercator, published an important map of the world in 1569. His map converted the features of the spherical Earth onto a flat surface using a system of projection. In a Mercator projection map, rhumb lines are shown as straight lines. Rhumb lines are lines that follow a single **compass** setting and make oblique, or indirect, angles with all the **meridians**, which represent the lines of longitude.

circumnavigation of Earth in 1522. By circling the world, his expedition uncovered the huge size of the Pacific Ocean and provided information about the diameter of Earth.

The Spanish Conquests

Spanish **conquistadores** explored parts of South, Central, and North America in the 1500s. In these new lands they saw an opportunity to gain new territories and colonize them. They also sought to obtain the riches of these lands and their peoples. The Spanish tried to subdue the native peoples and convert them to Christianity. Those who did not convert were threatened with death—this threat was often and brutally carried out.

Mapping the southern part of the Americas began in 1500 when Portuguese navigator Pedro Alvares Cabral crossed the southern Atlantic Ocean to reach Brazil, which he thought was an island. The Italian navigator Amerigo Vespucci, became the first to realize that the South American coast stretched unbroken from Venezuela to Argentina. Reaching Brazil in 1501, he named one of the bays *Rio de Janeiro*, which means "river of January."

Spanish conquistador Vasco Núñez de Balboa crossed the **Isthmus** of Panama in 1513 and was the first European to see the Pacific Ocean. Puerto Rico was conquered in 1508 by Spanish conquistador Juan Ponce de León, who then discovered Florida in 1513. Carib Indians prevented him from further conquest there, and he fled to Cuba where he soon died.

Pedro Alvares Cabral's visit to Brazil encouraged further exploration of the region.

Theatrum Orbis Terrarum

In 1570, Abraham Ortelius published one of the world's first modern atlases, or books of maps. His book contained seventy maps, and it was revised and updated several times.

The 1519 voyage of Spanish conquistador Hernando Cortés led to his discovery of Mexico, and then its tragic conquest and plunder for its gold. Exploration of the region resulted in Mexico appearing on European maps in 1526. It was called *Nueva Espana*, which means "New Spain." Another Spanish conquistador, Francisco Pizarro, conquered Peru during his expedition begun in 1528.

This map of New Spain was published in the Theatrum Orbis Terrarum, *one of the first modern atlases.*

King Louis XIV
began the mapping
of France by
ordering a detailed
survey of Paris.

Chapter Three

Mapping Nations

It is one thing to discover a country, but it is quite another thing to map it. Mapping an entire nation takes a lot of time, money, and labor. Few governments were willing to do this until France took up the challenge in the 1700s.

The mapping of France came about because of King Louis XIV's desire to make his nation the most technologically advanced in Europe. Part of this goal was to redesign the country with new roads, bridges, and canals that would be the best in the world. But before the nation could begin its construction projects, it had to be scientifically mapped.

The mapping of France began with a detailed survey of Paris. The king commissioned French astronomer Jean Picard to measure the arc, or curved line, of a meridian, which is one of the imaginary lines of longitude that form a half-circle from the North and South Poles. Meridian means "midday." Longitude is best understood and calculated as a function of time since the North-South lines of longitude mark time zones around the globe. Picard had to determine the starting point—the prime meridian upon which cartographers would base their maps of the nation.

To determine **latitude**, Picard viewed stars and Jupiter's moons through a telescope. The stars appear at a certain angle above the horizon. If you are standing at the equator, a star directly overhead is at a 90 degree angle to the ground. If you walk north until the star appears at an 89 degree angle to the ground, you have reached a latitude of 1 degree north. You can then tell how many miles you have traveled because there are 360 degrees in a circle, and then the **circumference** of Earth is approximately 24,000 miles. Each degree of latitude is one part in 360 of the whole circumference. Divide 24,000 miles by 360, and you can find out how many miles you walked.

To measure the surface of the city, the system of **triangulation**—using three angles—was used. This involved a surveyor measuring a line between two points, the baseline of an imaginary triangle. A distant landmark was chosen as the third

The King Is Not Pleased

King Louis XIV was unhappy after seeing the results of Jean Picard's boundary calculations of France. Upon seeing that the nation was not as large as he had thought, Louis cried out, "Your work has cost me a major portion of my realm!"

How Round Is the Earth?

Sir Isaac Newton, a British scientist, maintained that the Earth was not perfectly round. He believed it was slightly flat at the top and bottom (the North and South Poles). It also reputedly bulged out a little at the **equator**. He came to these conclusions after observing those properties of Jupiter and Saturn through his telescope.

Newton's theories alarmed mapmakers. If they were true, then degrees of longitude got longer at the poles. New scientifically drawn maps and globes would have to reflect Newton's less-than-round shape of the world. After extensive study, and scientific expeditions to Peru and Lapland to measure the length of a degree of latitude and determine the correct shape of the Earth, scientists concluded in 1737 that Newton had been right. The Earth was not round but flattened at the poles and bulged slightly at the equator.

This photograph shows the Cassini triangulation map of France published in 1744.

point of the triangle. By measuring the angles of the triangle at the baseline, the laws of geometry can be used to find the lengths of the other two sides. From this, it was learned how far away the baseline points were from the distant landmark.

Picard used astronomical sightings to accomplish more accurate triangular measurements that resulted in more accurate mapping. It was time-consuming, exhausting work. Between 1679 to 1681, after he finished surveying Paris, Picard and his associates mapped the French coastline.

The king entrusted the project of mapping France to an Italian. He was Giovanni Domenico Cassini, a cartographer and astronomer. The project was called the Carte de Cassini because four generations of the Cassini family worked on it until it was completed more than a century later.

A New Map of the World

While the mapping of France was stalled after the death of Picard, Cassini drew the most accurate map of the world up to that time. He placed nations, islands, and bodies of water according to astronomical observations that helped him determine their exact latitude and longitude. Cassini's map was 24 feet (7.3 meters) wide, so huge that it took up the entire floor of a tower in the Paris Observatory.

Cassini hired amateur surveyors all over the world to contribute data to his map. The map also included information contributed by professional surveyors in hundreds of European towns and cities. Published in 1696, Cassini's world map became the standard for world maps over the next century. The accomplishment enabled him to get the king's permission in 1700 to resume more scientific mapping of the nation of France after Picard's death.

A Family of Mapmakers

Generations of Cassini family worked on the mapping of France. Jean Dominique Cassini and his son Jacques produced a complete map of France in 1744, and mapped an accurate baseline from the Paris Observatory to Greenwich, England. In 1747, King Louis XV asked a third generation Cassini, César-Francois, to make an even more detailed map of France. This map was completed in 1759 by Jacques Dominique Cassini, great-grandson of the map's originator. The final map of France was published in 1793. The map was on 182 sheets of paper and when it was assembled it formed a 36-foot (11-meter) square. Its military, political, and economic value was immediately recognized.

Jean Dominique Cassini and his son would be the ones to finish mapping France.

Only a year later, the French Revolution broke out. Citizens demanded equality and the heads of the aristocracy. Cassini was one of the few of the privileged class whose head did not get chopped off by the guillotine. He was later honored by Emperor Napoleon Bonaparte, who used the Cassini maps in his administration and as a tool of conquest.

England, Austria, and Germany soon followed France in conducting their own national surveys. Mapping of Norway and Sweden began in 1815 and of Russia a year later. Denmark and Switzerland began their national mapping programs in 1830.

Mapping England

The mapping of England began largely because of the determination of William Roy, a major general in the British army. Failing to get support for a national survey from King George III or his government, he began the project on his own. Walking the countryside for triangulation routes in 1784, he measured a baseline as a start.

The Royal Society then put Roy in charge of the British side of a joint project with the French academy, Academie Francaise. His job was to oversee the London-Dover survey of the English Channel. The king, very interested in science, visited Roy at work and became so fascinated that he promised his full support in mapping the entire country. The timing also was right. Funds for the project would be available since the Revolutionary War had ended and would no longer drain the national treasury.

One of the greatest achievements in the surveying of England was the invention of the **theodolite**. Roy commissioned inventor and instrument-maker Jesse Ramsden to design an advanced surveying instrument for measuring both

Unlike King Louis XIV of France, King George III of Great Britain had no interest in mapping his lands at first.

These are two instruments used in surveying. On the left is a theodolite, which is used to determine altitude. On the right is a circumferentor, sometimes called a survey's compass, which takes horizontal angles and bearings.

horizontal and **vertical** angles to within fractions of a second of arc. Ramsden's invention, the theodolite, was a device with a brass circle fitted with fine-adjustment attachments, telescopes, and lanterns for night observations.

The theodolite helped in the successful surveying of the English Channel, but Roy—in order to win his commission to map all of England—had to resort to another type of device. This he did by challenging the national pride, telling officials that the English should have at least as good a map of their country as the French had of theirs. The verbal device worked. He got the job, and England was put on the map.

Mapping the United States

During colonial times, surveyors Joshua Fry and Peter Jefferson mapped the region from Virginia to the Great Lakes in 1751. Four years later, John Mitchell, a Virginia colonist, compiled a *Map of the British and French Dominions in America*. It was used to mark the boundaries of the United States after the Revolutionary War.

More than forty years later, large sections of the American West were explored and mapped. President Thomas Jefferson sent Meriwether Lewis and William Clark to explore the new land acquired by the nation in the Louisiana Purchase and find a water route to the Pacific Ocean. Beginning their trip in 1804, they took two years to complete their journey, which resulted in a master map that included longitude and latitude for vast regions of terrain. Their expedition was aided by their female American Indian guide, Sacagawea, and other local Indians who drew rough maps for them of territories that lay ahead on the journey.

As pioneers moved westward in the mid-1800s, explorers and army engineers mapped trails and surveyed the land. Soon

Washington the Mapmaker

George Washington decided to become a mapmaker when he was sixteen, assisting two surveyors mapping Virginia in 1748. During the Revolutionary War, General Washington drew maps for military campaigns, including one he called "Plan of a line of march in a forest country."

This photograph shows a map drawn in William Clark's journal.

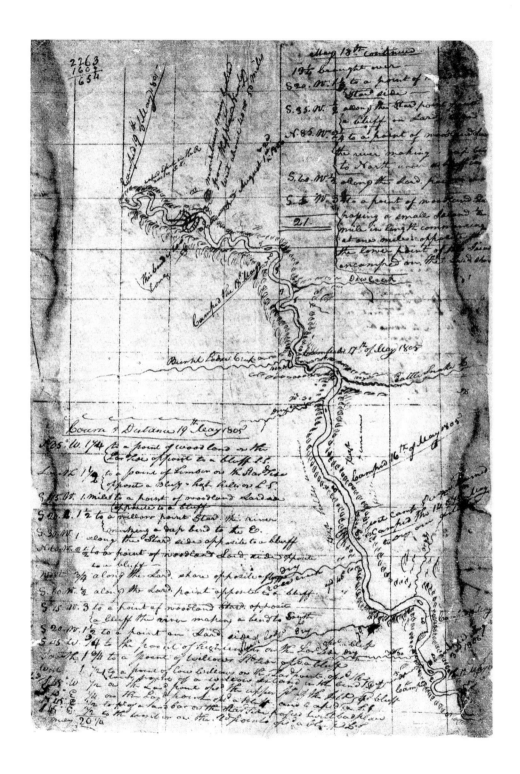

The Mountain Men

Among the earliest explorer-map-makers of America were adventurers known as Mountain Men. They roamed the western mountain ranges, trapping beaver and other animals to obtain fur pelts, often mapping territories along the way. Among the most famous was Jedediah Smith, who journeyed west with Canadian fur trader Alexander Ross. They became the first European men to cross the Sierra Nevada mountain range and the Great Salt Lake Desert into California. Smith's travels, in harsh weather and hostile American Indian country, helped blaze trails and open territories for eventual settlement all the way to the Pacific Ocean.

the territories west of Pennsylvania were opened for settlement as townships, roads, rivers, and mountain ranges were mapped. Two government agencies were established to survey the United States. They were the U.S. Coast Survey, founded in 1807 (now the National Oceanic and Atmospheric Administration), and the U.S. Geological Survey, created in 1879.

The last part of the United States to be explored and charted was Alaska. The territory was 615,230 square miles (1,593,438 square kilometers) in size. It was purchased from Russia in 1867 for $7.2 million or about two cents an acre. First thought to be a worthless frozen wasteland of snow and ice, Alaska was later surveyed and found to be rich in coal, natural gas, oil, fur, timber, wildlife, and farmland.

Before exploring the Pacific Ocean, James Cook spent four years surveying the coasts of Labrador, Newfoundland, and Nova Scotia.

Chapter Four

Mapping the Unknown

While some people focused on creating better, more accurate maps of known countries, others chose to explore and map miles of uncharted land and sea. In the 1700s, voyages to discover and explore vast regions of the Pacific led to the creation of new and more accurate maps of the world. British Captain James Cook explored the Pacific Ocean on his voyages between 1768 and 1771, charting the east coast of Australia and the main islands of New Zealand. In 1773 he became the first person to cross the Antarctic Circle, and in 1778 he discovered the islands called Hawai'i. His voyages gathered new information that helped mapmakers.

The North and South Poles

Among the last places on Earth to be reached, explored, and mapped were its most remote—the North and South Poles. However, some expeditions had come close to them as early as the 1500s and recorded some knowledge of them. These included Barents' expedition to north Norway in 1596, Bering's explorations north of Alaska in 1725, Cook's voyage to the Antarctic Circle in 1773, and British voyages to investigate the oceans in 1872.

Through these and other expeditions, geographers had some knowledge of the polar regions and cartographers had mapped the **boundaries** of the Arctic and Antarctic by the late 1800s. But no one had yet reached either the North or South Pole. It was a challenge few nations or adventurers could resist, and a race to the poles began early in the 1900s.

The North Pole is the northernmost place on Earth, a vast, permanently frozen wilderness floating in icy seas. Dutch navigator Willem Barents never reached it in his voyages exploring the sea north of Norway, now called the Barents Sea. When his ship was ice-locked in the frozen Arctic sea, he and his crew survived a severe winter in a cabin they built from their ship's wood, but he died on the journey home the following spring. Nearly three hundred years later, American

This illustration is from a book on Barents' travels.

publisher Charles Hall died on his third unsuccessful attempt to reach the North Pole by dogsled.

In the early 1900s, two adventurers raced each other to be the first to reach the North Pole. They were two Americans, navy officer Robert E. Peary and explorer-surgeon Dr. Frederick Cook. Cook claimed he reached the North Pole first in April 1908, with two Inuit Indian guides. A year later Peary made the same claim. He said he had reached the North Pole on his eighth attempt, by dogsled and with five companions, on April 6, 1909.

A lengthy investigation followed. Cook had no proof of his claim, but Peary produced photos he had taken and reports he had written as he surveyed the polar region. Also, Peary's guides supported his claim, while Cook's did not. In 1911, the U.S. Congress declared Peary had reached the North Pole first.

In more recent years, the matter of who in Peary's group reached the North Pole first on April 6, 1909, became further clarified. Peary was the first white man to reach the North Pole, but his African-American assistant, Matthew Henson, actually had gotten to the Pole before him. Peary arrived 45 minutes later with four Inuits. While geographic expeditions to both the North and South Poles have continued over the years, because of the harshness of their weather the poles remain two of the least-charted areas on earth.

Robert Peary tried to reach the North Pole seven times before his successful expedition in 1909.

Even harsher conditions faced those who attempted to reach the South Pole. They not only braved similar freezing weather but encountered high mountains to scale and treacherous crevasses underfoot. Captain Robert Scott led a British scientific expedition in the Antarctic between 1901 and 1904. He returned to the Antarctic in 1910 intent on reaching the

South Pole. But a rival Norwegian explorer, Roald Amundsen, reached it first, on December 14, 1911. On their way back to camp, Scott and his men were trapped in a fierce snowstorm and died. Months later, their frozen bodies were discovered. Ironically, Amundsen died at the North Pole while attempting to rescue another explorer in 1928.

Mountains to Climb

The 1800s and 1900s were years of climbing great mountains. These climbing expeditions resulted in the mapping of previously uncharted regions of the world. The most exciting adventures took place in the highest reaches mountaineers could climb.

One of the greatest mountain-climbing adventures was the conquest of the world's highest mountain, Peak XV in the Himalayas, on the border of Tibet and Nepal. In 1856 it was named Mount Everest in honor of Sir George Everest of Great Britain who had surveyed both India and the Himalayas. Eight attempts to scale the mountain failed over the next one hundred years.

The Everest expedition that proved successful was led by

*Many expeditions
failed in their efforts
to reach the top of
Mount Everest.*

Edmund Hillary, a New Zealand mountaineer. He left England in February 1953 and, with a small party of Nepalese Sherpa guides, began climbing up the south face of the mountain in May. Their first attempt to reach the top failed on May 26 because of a lack of oxygen.

Hillary and one Nepalese Sherpa guide, Tenzing Norgay, attempted a second effort three days later. After a grueling five-hour climb, they reached the top of Mount Everest shortly before noon on May 29. They stayed atop the mountain in the frigid air and blowing wind for only fifteen minutes while Hillary snapped pictures with his camera as Norgay planted the flags of Britain, Nepal, India, and the United Nations.

Tenzing Norgay (left) and Edmund Hillary (right) pose for a photograph after being honored by the king of Nepal.

The invention of the telegraph helped John Wesley Powell survey the Colorado River.

Chapter Five

Mapping the Modern World

In the 1800s and 1900s, three major technological advances helped cartographers draw more detailed maps. They were invention of the electric telegraph, photography, and the airplane. Telegraphic time signals from an astronomical station in Salt Lake City, Utah, gave precise data that helped John Wesley Powell compute longitude when he surveyed the Colorado River in 1869. Photographs of remote areas such as mountain ranges and canyons in the Rocky Mountains provided cartographers with image information they needed. The invention of the first successful airplane by the Wright Brothers in 1903 led to **aerial photography**, which provided pictures used for more detailed mapping.

Mapping Tools of Today

New technology continues to improve the way maps are made. **Remote-sensing photography** is an important new mapping method that utilizes electronic sensors and **radar** to gather and record geographic information from great distances. High-altitude photography produces amazingly detailed maps, allowing the camera to zoom in from photographing an entire city to photograph a street or a building on that street.

This photograph of the Middle East was taken by GPS satellite.

Mapmakers can pinpoint any location on Earth or track moving objects anywhere on the planet by means of the **Global Positioning System (GPS)**. GPS is a network of twenty-four **satellites** and receivers equipped with highly accurate clocks and computers. The satellite computers constantly beam coded signals reporting their positions to receiving stations on Earth. The receivers calculate their distance from the satellite. When four orbiting satellites beam down their location information, the receiver can calculate its exact position on Earth.

The United States also has Landsat satellites orbiting the Earth. These satellites take photographs of the planet that help make maps and provide visual evidence of a wide range of environmental concerns, such as crop growth, drought areas, and the location of forest fires. They also show atmospheric pollution and can locate underground oil sources. Detailed mapping, largely using various means of photography from space, continues to this day.

Cartographers Today

Even though much of the Earth has been mapped, cartographers are still very busy. They compile geographic, political, and cultural information and prepare maps of large areas for government agencies or private companies. Their work measuring, mapping, and charting the Earth's surface involves everything from geographical research and data compilation to actual map production.

Cartographers collect, analyze, and interpret two kinds of data. **Spatial data** involves latitude, longitude, elevation, and distance. **Nonspatial data** includes population density, land-use patterns, annual rainfall levels, and demographic characteristics. **Demographics** is the statistical study of human populations with regard to age, education, occupation,

A cartographer uses a computer to make a map.

International Map of the World

Work began on an international map of the world in 1891, but it was never completed. It was to be the most accurate and up-to-date map of national boundaries and resources at the time, but the project was halted after some nations resisted cooperating for reasons of national security.

income, and other categories. Cartographers prepare maps in either digital or graphic form. They gather information from mathematical surveys, laser beams, aerial photographs, and satellite data, then use computer technology to draw the maps.

Careers related to **cartography** include **photogrammetry**, map editing, and land surveying. Photogrammetrists prepare detailed maps and drawings from aerial photographs, usually of areas that are difficult or impossible to reach by other methods. Map editors develop and verify map contents from aerial photographs and other reference sources. Land survey-ors establish official land, airspace, and water boundaries. They write descriptions of land for deeds, leases, and other legal documents. They define airspace for airports and measure construction and mineral sites. Land surveyors man-age survey teams that measure distances, directions, angles between points, elevations of points, lines, and contours on the Earth's surface. Survey technicians assist land surveyors by operating survey instruments and collecting information.

Around 110,000 cartographers, photogrammetrists, surveyors, and surveying technicians were employed in the United States in 1998. About 64 percent worked for engineering and architectural services firms. Most of the rest were employed by federal, state, or local government agencies.

Private companies employing cartographers and surveyors include construction firms, mining, oil, and gas extraction companies, and public utilities. Major federal government employers of cartographers and surveyors are the U.S. Geological Survey, the Bureau of Land Management, the U.S. Army Corps of Engineers, the U.S. Forest Service, the National Oceanic and Atmospheric Administration, and the National Imagery and Mapping Agency. Most state and local government cartographers and surveyors work for highway departments and urban planning and redevelopment agencies.

A surveyor takes measurements.

Orienteering

In orienteering, you need to use a compass and a map to find your way to different places.

A fun way to learn about maps and how to use them is to take up the sport of **orienteering**. It began in Norway in the late 1800s as a way to learn to read maps. Today there are hundreds of orienteering clubs in the United States, Canada, and other countries.

Participants use a map, compass, and list of geographical clues to help them find their way from one point to another in a local or cross-country setting. The terrain is varied and usually wooded, requiring the crossing of streams and hills. Orienteering can be done on foot, bicycle, or skis.

The object of orienteering is to find your way as fast as possible from the starting to the finishing point, following a series of control points. Winners are those who best know all aspects of map reading. These include orientation, scale, direction, and symbols.

Timeline

550	Greek geographer Anaximander creates an early world map.
500	Hecataeus writes travel book, *Journey Around the World*.
444	Herodotus writes *The Histories*.
300s	Alexander the Great conquers Persian Empire. Pytheas sails around British Isles. Crates of Thebes makes a globe showing four continents.
240	Greek mathematician Eratosthenes estimates circumference of Earth.
115	The Silk Road opens trade between China and the West.

A.D.

10–20	Greek Strabo assembles a world geographic history.
100	Romans survey parts of Europe.
150	Greek astronomer Ptolemy creates a set of books called *Geography*.
1155	Earliest printed map is made in China.
1200s	Portolan navigation charts are first drawn.
1271–1296	Marco Polo travels to China and India.
1300s	Ptolemy's world map is rediscovered in Europe.
1436–1437	Johann Gutenberg invents printing with movable type.
1472	First map is produced on a printing press.
1492	Christopher Columbus sails to North America on October 12. Martin Behaim creates first globe in Western world.
1499	Amerigo Vespucci sails to West Indies.
1522	Ferdinand Magellan's expedition completes the first circumnavigation of Earth.

(continued)

Timeline (continued)

1526	Mexico appears on a European map.
1679–1681	Paris and the coastline of France are mapped.
1700–1793	The Cassini family produces detailed maps of France.
1748	George Washington surveys Virginia.
1755	John Mitchell compiles *Map of the British and French Dominions in America*.
1762	John Harrison's chronometer makes it possible to determine accurate longitude at sea.
1768–1771	Captain James Cook explores the Pacific Ocean.
1780s	England is mapped.
1804–1806	Meriwether Lewis and William Clark explore and map Louisiana Territory from Missouri to the Pacific Ocean.
1807	Thomas Jefferson establishes U.S. Coast Survey (now the National Oceanic and Atmospheric Administration).
1879	U.S. Geological Survey is established.
1909	Robert E. Peary and Matthew Henson reach the North Pole on April 6.
1911	Roald Amundsen reaches the South Pole on December 14.
1953	Edmund Hillary climbs Mt. Everest in Nepal on May 29.
1972	Landsat satellites are launched by United States to aid in mapmaking from space.
1978	Global Positioning System begins, providing satellite surveying from space orbit.
1984	France's SPOT satellite is launched to provide detailed surveying of Earth.

Glossary

aerial photography—taking overlapping photos of the ground from airplanes for mapping purposes

boundary—a line that marks the limit of one place, such as a state or country, and another

Buddhism—a religion based on the teachings of Buddha

cartographer—a person who draws, plans, and studies maps

cartography—the making and studying of maps

circumference—the distance around the rim or perimeter of a circle

circumnavigate—to sail around

compass—a navigational instrument for determining direction by showing where north is

conquistador—a person who conquers

demographics—the statistical study of populations with regard to age, income, occupation, and other characteristics

equator—the imaginary line circling the Earth at latitude zero degrees. The starting point for measuring north and south on a map or globe.

gazetteer—a geographical dictionary

Global Positioning System—a system whereby surveying information is beamed from satellites to receivers on Earth

globe—a sphere on which a map of the Earth or sky is depicted

horizontal—lines that are parallel to ground level

isthmus—a narrow strip of land that lies between two bodies of water

latitude—how far a place is to the north and south of the equator

longitude—how far a place is to the east or west of the prime meridian

map—a drawing, usually on a flat surface, of part or all of the surface of the Earth or sky

meridian—a line of longitude running north and south on a globe

nonspatial data—information, such as population and rainfall statistics

orienteering—the sport of finding one's way using map and compass

photogrammetry—the science of making measurements through the use of aerial photographs

portolan chart—a medieval chart that helped sailors reach their destinations at sea

prime meridian—an imaginary line that runs through Greenwich, England, marking the line of zero degrees longitude

radar—a detecting device utilizing radio waves

remote-sensing photography—a method for mapping from great distances

satellite—a human-made object launched from and orbiting Earth

spatial data—information such as location, elevation, distance

survey—collecting information about the land by measuring its size and shape

theodolite—a surveying instrument

triangulation—a measurement of three angles

vertical—lines that are in an upright position

To Find Out More

Books

Blandford, Percy W. *The New Explorer's Guide to Maps and Compasses*. Blue Ridge Summit, PA: Tab Books, 1992.

Bramwell, Martyn. *How Maps Are Made*. Minneapolis, MN: Lerner, 1998.

Brewer, Paul. *Explorers and Exploration: Vol. 2: The Golden Age of Exploration*. Danbury, CT: Grolier, 1998.

Ganeri, Anita. *The Story of Maps and Navigation*. New York: Oxford University Press, 1997.

Harris, Nathaniel. *Explorers and Exploration: Vol. 1: The Earliest Explorers*. Danbury, CT: Grolier, 1998.

Johnson, Sylvia A. *Mapping the World*. New York: Atheneum, 1999.

Lerangis, Peter. *Journey to the Pole: Antarctica*. New York: Scholastic, 2000.

Pratt, Paula Bryant. *Maps: Plotting Places on the Globe*. San Diego, CA: Lucent Books, 1995.

Organizations and Online Sites

Ancient History: Maps
http://ancienthistory.about.com
This online site offers a wealth of information on maps and geography of the ancient world.

History of Cartography
University of Minnesota
2221 University Avenue SE
Minneapolis, MN 55414
http://www.-map.lib.umn/history_of_cartography.html
The John R. Borchert map library at the University of Minnesota offers extensive information about maps throughout history.

International Orienteering Federation

http://www.orienteering.org

This organization provides information on the sport of orienteering.

National Oceanic and Atmospheric Administration

http://www.nnic.noaa.gov

This online site offers information from NOAA's Network Information Center.

Occupational Outlook Handbook

http://stats.bls.gov/oco/ocos040.html

This online site provides information from U.S. Department of Labor publications on careers for cartographers, photogrammetrists, and surveying technicians.

U.S. Geological Survey

http://www.usgs.gov

This government agency's online site allows visitors to access information on mapping, geology, and educational resources in cartography.

A Note on Sources

I've always loved studying maps. When I was a boy growing up during World War II, I used to draw my own smaller-scale versions of full-page maps in the newspapers. Each day, they showed where the war was being fought in Europe, the Pacific, or Africa. I learned a great deal about world geography that way and developed a lifelong fascination with maps. I papered my college dormitory room with *National Geographic* maps, covering the ceiling as well as the walls.

When I research to write a book, I try to combine library research with contacting experts on the subject. In researching this book I had to rely primarily on libraries. I got the help of research librarians at four nearby libraries in Chicago, Evanston, Wilmette, and Glenview, Illinois. They recommended both adult and juvenile books on map history and I began by reading those for young readers, then graduated to the adult books. For young readers, I found the most helpful basic books on map history to be Nathaniel Harris's *The Earliest Explorers*, Paul Brewer's *The Golden Age of Exploration*, Alma Graham's *Discovering Maps*, and Ray Broekel's *Maps and Globes*. The most helpful adult books on map history were Norman Thrower's *Maps and Civilization*, David Woodward's *The History of Cartography*, and Peter Whitfield's *New Found Lands, Maps in the History of Exploration*.

I also sit at my computer and go online to surf the World Wide Web for sites to help me research a subject. For researching the history of maps, online sites listed in the To Find Out More section were especially helpful.

I always find researching a subject to be fascinating because it never fails that I learn even more than I thought I would. It's really fun to share with readers little-known, often exciting, and sometimes funny things I find, such as those I include in this book about the adventures and dangers both men and women encountered on their mapmaking expeditions.

—*Walter Oleksy*

Index

Numbers in *italics* indicate illustrations.

About the Author

Walter Oleksy has been a freelance writer of books, mostly for young readers, for more than twenty-five years. He came to that occupation after several years as a newspaper reporter for *The Chicago Tribune* and as editor of three feature and travel magazines. A native of Chicago, he received a bachelor of arts degree in journalism from Michigan State University, then was editor of a U.S. Army newspaper for two years before starting his writing career.

He lives in a Chicago suburb with his best friend Max, a mix of Labrador retriever and German shepherd. They take frequent walks in the nearby woods and swim in Lake Michigan.

His most recent book for Children's Press is *The Philippines*. His other books for young readers include *Hispanic-American Scientists* and *American Military Leaders of World War II*.